Creative
CHRISTMAS
Parties

Compiled by Laura Demse.

ISBN 978-1-61626-382-9

All scripture quotations are taken from the King James Version of the Bible.

Published by Barbour Publishing, Inc., P.O. Box 719, Uhrichsville, Ohio 44683, www.barbourbooks.com

Our mission is to publish and distribute inspirational products offering exceptional value and biblical encouragement to the masses.

Member of the
Evangelical Christian
Publishers Association

Printed in China.

Creative
CHRISTMAS
Parties

Recipes & Inspiration for Your Holiday Event

BARBOUR
PUBLISHING

Welcome to *Creative Christmas Parties*! Here you'll find a plethora of tasty recipes, festive inspiration, and ideas to make your holiday get-togethers truly merry and bright. Each page is a stand-alone recipe card that can be easily removed from the book to add to your collection of other holiday treats; or you may choose to share some of the cards with friends and family. Consider creating the dish to give as a gift and attaching the recipe card with a bright ribbon. Or maybe slip a recipe card or two into your Christmas cards this year. You may also wish to keep the book as a whole—no matter how you use it, you can't go wrong!

Recipes are organized in colorful sections:

Bountiful Beginnings: Appetizers

The Festive Feast: Main Dishes

All the Trimmings: Sides

Confection Celebration: Desserts

Creative Christmas: Favors, Decorating Ideas, Party Games

Bountiful Beginnings: Appetizers

Appetizers set the stage for every party—large and small. Get creative in your presentation of these appetizers by selecting a colorful variety of dishes to whet guests' appetites. Bring out your fancy serving platters for presentation and unbox your punch bowl for a touch of flair. Arrange platters of appetizers on the coffee table along with plates and napkins for easy self-service. Low lamplight and candles around the room will relax and delight your guests, who are no doubt a bit harried this time of year. Encourage them to kick off their shoes and sit on the floor if they'd like.

And all the bells on earth shall ring,
On Christmas Day, on Christmas Day,
And all the bells on earth shall ring,
On Christmas Day in the morning.

TRADITIONAL ENGLISH CAROL

Christmas Punch

4 oranges
3 lemons
1 quart pineapple juice
2 cups cranberry juice cocktail
2 quarts cold water
8 tablespoons loose tea or 16 tea bags

4 large cinnamon sticks
1 tablespoon whole cloves
1 teaspoon whole allspice
½ cup sugar
2 quarts sweet apple cider
2 (2 liter) bottles extra dry ginger ale

Wash fruit. Squeeze juice from oranges and lemons into large bowl, removing seeds. Add rinds to bowl. Add pineapple juice and cranberry juice cocktail; set aside. In large saucepan, bring water to a full boil. If using loose tea, place it in a tea ball or tie it in a cheesecloth bag with spices. If using tea bags, put spices in tea ball or tie in cheesecloth bag. Add tea and spices to boiling water, let steep for 10 minutes. Remove tea and spices and discard them. Add combined rinds and fruit juices, sugar, and apple cider to saucepan. Bring to a boil, stirring constantly. Strain punch into slow cooker set on low heat. Just before serving, gently stir in ginger ale. The punch should be served very warm. Yield: approximately 2 gallons

Tip: If serving punch from a punch bowl instead of a slow cooker, place a large metal spoon in the bowl before adding hot liquids to help prevent the bowl from breaking.

FESTIVE BEVERAGES

These festive nonalcoholic beverages are perfect for the holidays.

Mock Champagne Cocktail

2 cups lemon juice
2 cups pomegranate syrup or
   grenadine syrup

2 cups apricot nectar
2 to 4 bottles nonalcoholic sparkling
   white grape juice or sparkling cider

Make sure all ingredients are chilled. Pour lemon juice into large serving pitcher or punch bowl. Stir in pomegranate syrup and apricot nectar, blending well. Gently stir in sparkling juice or cider. Add crushed ice, if desired. Serve in punch glasses or champagne flutes. Yield: approximately 10 to 12 servings

Mock Pink Champagne Punch

3 (6 ounce) cans frozen lemonade
   concentrate
1 cup pomegranate syrup or grenadine
   syrup, chilled
1 (2 liter) bottle extra dry ginger ale,
   chilled

2 quarts tonic or quinine water, chilled
1 quart sherbet, slightly defrosted
   (raspberry, lemon, or pineapple is good)
1 lemon, thinly sliced
1 lime, thinly sliced
Fresh mint leaves, optional

Slightly thaw lemonade concentrate. Just before serving, pour thawed lemonade concentrate into large punch bowl. Stir in pomegranate syrup and blend well. Gently stir in ginger ale and tonic water. Finally, add sherbet in small scoops to float on top. Garnish with fresh lemon and lime slices and mint leaves, if desired. Serve in punch glasses or champagne flutes. Yield: approximately 24 servings.

Carrot Soup

This colorful, flavorful soup is wonderful year round.

2 tablespoons olive oil
1½ cups chopped onions
2 cloves garlic, finely minced
1 teaspoon grated fresh ginger
1 teaspoon cumin
¼ teaspoon cayenne pepper
1 teaspoon salt
2 pounds carrots, peeled and cut into
  ¼-inch slices

2 medium potatoes, peeled and diced
5 cups vegetable or chicken stock
½ cup orange juice
3 tablespoons peanut butter
1 tablespoon fresh parsley, chopped for
  garnish

Heat oil in large stockpot over medium heat. Add onions, garlic, ginger, cumin, and cayenne pepper, stirring to blend well. Sauté until onions are soft, about 8 to 10 minutes. Stir in salt, and then add carrots, potatoes, and stock. Bring mixture to a boil. Reduce heat to low and simmer until vegetables are tender, about 25 to 30 minutes. Remove from heat and stir in orange juice and peanut butter. Working in small batches, carefully puree the soup in food processor or blender until smooth. Transfer soup to warmed serving tureen or slow cooker set on low to keep warm. Serve in warmed mugs or bowls. Garnish with parsley before serving, if desired.

Notes

Onion Soup with Caramelized Onions

The caramelized onions for this soup can be made and kept refrigerated in an airtight container up to 1 week or frozen for up to 2 months.

2 pounds sweet onions, halved and thickly sliced
¼ cup olive oil or butter

2 cups beef, chicken, or vegetable stock, undiluted

Combine sweet onions, oil or butter, and stock in slow cooker, stirring to mix. Cook covered on high temperature for 8 hours or until onion slices are golden brown and very soft. Use immediately or refrigerate or freeze until needed.

Yield: 2 cups

2 cups sweet caramelized onions (recipe above)

2 cups beef consommé, undiluted

2 cups beef, chicken, or vegetable stock, undiluted

2 cups water

½ teaspoon dried thyme

¼ cup white or red wine, optional*

1½ to 2 cups croutons

1 cup shredded swiss or gruyère cheese

Combine caramelized onions, consommé, stock, water, and thyme in slow cooker; blending well. Stir in wine, if using. Cook covered on high for 2½ to 3 hours. Serve soup in warmed mugs or bowls. Top each with some of the croutons and shredded cheese, if desired. Yield: 12 mug servings or 6 bowl servings.

*NOTE: The wine in this recipe is added before cooking, so the alcohol will dissipate before serving. If you prefer not to cook with alcohol, the wine can be omitted and the soup will still be delicious.

Spiced Snack Nuts

Nuts are a healthy treat, and making these specialty spiced nuts at home is fun and easy. Store them in airtight containers. They make wonderful gifts as well!

Orange Spiced Walnuts

3 cups sugar
1 cup orange juice
2 teaspoons grated orange zest

1 teaspoon pure vanilla extract
1 teaspoon ground cinnamon
6 cups walnut halves

Butter a baking sheet or line it with waxed paper; set aside. In saucepan, combine sugar and orange juice. Bring to a boil on medium-high heat.
Cook until temperature reaches the soft ball stage or 240 degrees on candy

thermometer. Remove saucepan from heat. Stir in orange zest, vanilla, cinnamon, and walnuts. Stir mixture until syrup begins to look cloudy. Before mixture hardens, spoon it onto prepared baking sheet. Separate nuts and let them cool completely. Yield: approximately 2 pounds

Honey Pecans

3 tablespoons melted butter
¼ cup brown sugar, packed
¼ cup honey
½ teaspoon salt

½ teaspoon ground cinnamon
¼ teaspoon ground cardamom
¼ teaspoon ground allspice
3 cups pecan halves

Butter a baking sheet or line it with parchment paper; set aside. Preheat oven to 325 degrees. In bowl, stir together butter, brown sugar, honey, salt, cinnamon, cardamom, and allspice. Add pecan halves and toss them to coat nuts with spice mix. Spread mixture onto prepared baking sheet. Bake for 20 minutes. Transfer to rack to cool completely.

Cheese Crackers

2 cups shredded swiss or cheddar
  cheese
½ cup grated parmesan cheese
½ cup butter, softened

3 tablespoons water
1 cup flour
¼ teaspoon salt
1 cup rolled oats

Beat cheeses, butter, and water with electric mixer until well blended. Mix in flour, salt, and oats, blending until thoroughly combined. Shape dough into a 12-inch long roll, wrap firmly in plastic wrap; refrigerate at least 4 hours. Preheat oven to 400 degrees. Cut into ¼-inch thick slices and place them on parchment-lined or greased baking sheets. Bake for 8 to 10 minutes until golden brown. Transfer to wire racks to cool. Yield: 4 dozen

Notes

....

....

....

....

....

....

....

Appetizer Puffs

Fill with salads, spreads, and dips.
A cheese variation is given below the basic recipe.

1 cup flour	½ cup butter
½ teaspoon salt	4 large eggs
1 cup water	

Line baking sheet with parchment paper; set aside. Mix flour and salt together in bowl; set aside. In saucepan, bring water and butter to a boil. Stir in dry ingredients with a wooden spoon. Beat until mixture leaves the sides of pan and forms a ball. Remove from heat. Add eggs, one at a time, beating well after each. With a scoop or spoon, shape dough into walnut-sized balls; place on prepared baking sheet. Bake at 400 degrees for 20 to 25 minutes until brown and dry. Carefully slice the top third off each puff. Fill, place tops back on; transfer to serving dish. Yield: 18 puffs

Appetizer Cheese Puffs

1 cup flour
½ teaspoon salt
⅛ teaspoon cayenne pepper
⅛ teaspoon dry mustard

1 cup water
½ cup butter
4 large eggs
¾ cup grated swiss or cheddar cheese

Line baking sheets with parchment paper; set aside. Mix flour, salt, cayenne pepper, and dry mustard together in bowl; set aside. In saucepan, bring water and butter to a boil. Stir in dry ingredients with a wooden spoon. Beat until mixture leaves the sides of the pan and forms a ball. Remove from heat. Add eggs, beating well after each. Beat in cheese. Shape the dough into walnut-sized balls; place on prepared baking sheets. Bake at 400 degrees for 20 to 25 minutes until brown and dry. Carefully slice the top third off each puff. Fill, place tops back on; transfer to serving dish. Yield: 36 puffs

CANDACE'S SEA-LICIOUS CRAB SPREADS

*Serve these delicious crab spreads with
assorted crackers, sliced breads, or fresh vegetables.*

Crab and Shrimp Spread

- 1 (8 ounce) package cream cheese, softened
- 2 to 3 teaspoons light cream, half-and-half, or milk
- 1 (6 to 8 ounce) package crabmeat, thawed and drained, if frozen

- ½ cup shrimp, finely chopped
- ½ teaspoon dried marjoram, crushed
- ¼ cup finely chopped onion
- Pinch salt
- Freshly ground black pepper

Place cream cheese in bowl. Gradually mix in enough light cream until mixture is smooth but not thin. Flake crabmeat. Stir crabmeat and shrimp into cheese mixture. Stir in marjoram, onion, salt, and pepper. Spoon mixture into lightly greased baking dish. Bake at 375 degrees for 15 to 20 minutes until heated through.

Layered Spicy Crabmeat Spread

¼ cup dry minced onion
¼ cup milk
2 (8 ounce) packages cream cheese, softened

2 (6 to 8 ounce) packages crabmeat, thawed and drained, if frozen
1 (12 ounce) bottle chili sauce
1½ cups ketchup
½ to 1 teaspoon hot pepper sauce

Soak dry onion in the milk for 15 minutes, until softened. Mix together onion and cream cheese and place mixture into serving dish with a rim. Flake crabmeat and distribute over cream cheese layer. Mix together chili sauce, ketchup, and hot pepper sauce and spoon it over crabmeat layer. Cover and chill well before serving.

Sauerkraut Sausage Balls

8 ounces pork sausage, finely crumbled
¼ cup finely chopped onion
14 ounces sauerkraut, well drained and
  snipped into small pieces
2 tablespoons dry fine bread crumbs
⅓ cup cream cheese, softened
2 tablespoons finely chopped fresh parsley

1 teaspoon prepared mustard
¼ teaspoon garlic powder
¼ teaspoon pepper
¼ cup flour
2 eggs, well beaten
¼ cup milk or water
¾ cup dry fine bread crumbs

In frying pan, cook sausage and onions until meat is browned. Remove from heat and drain fat. Add sauerkraut and 2 tablespoons bread crumbs to sausage onion mixture, stirring well to combine. In large bowl, combine cream cheese, parsley, mustard, garlic powder, and pepper until well blended.

Stir in sauerkraut mixture. Cover and chill for 2 to 3 hours in refrigerator. Set up 3 shallow dishes; put flour in one dish. In another, combine the eggs and milk. In the third dish, put ¾ cup bread crumbs. When sauerkraut sausage mixture is thoroughly chilled, shape into ¾-inch balls. Roll each ball into flour, then the egg mixture, and finally in bread crumbs. Fry in a little oil just to brown the balls, drain on brown paper or paper toweling.* To prepare for serving, place sauerkraut balls on baking sheet and bake at 400 degrees for 20 to 25 minutes. Transfer to warm platter. Serve alone or with a selection of cheeses.

NOTE: The balls can be frozen at this point for up to 3 months. If frozen, thaw to room temperature before baking as directed above.

Crab Stuffed Mushrooms

Traditionally served as an appetizer,
these mushrooms can also be served as a side dish.

24 large, fresh button mushrooms
¼ cup vegetable oil
2 (6 to 8 ounce) packages crabmeat,
  thawed and drained, if frozen
2 eggs, lightly beaten

¼ cup mayonnaise
¼ cup onion, finely chopped
1 tablespoon lemon juice
1 cup soft fine bread crumbs, divided
¼ cup butter, melted

Preheat oven to 375 degrees. Lightly butter a baking dish large enough to hold all the mushrooms in an upright position. Rinse mushrooms and pat dry with toweling. Depending on the mushroom, you may find it helpful to cut off a small slice on the bottom of each so that they will stand up in the baking dish and on a serving platter. Remove stems and save them for future use in soups or stews or discard them. Brush mushroom caps lightly with vegetable oil. Place them into prepared baking dish. In bowl, combine crabmeat, eggs, mayonnaise, onion, lemon juice, and half of the bread crumbs. Mix until thoroughly blended. Fill each of the mushrooms evenly with crabmeat mixture. Combine remaining bread crumbs with melted butter. Top each filled mushroom with a portion of bread crumb topping. Bake mushrooms for 15 minutes. Transfer to warm serving platter, if desired. Yield: 24 mushroom appetizers

Yummy Shrimp

1½ cups butter or extra-virgin olive oil
1 onion, finely chopped
4 cloves garlic, finely minced
1 tablespoon dried rosemary, crushed
3 tablespoons Worcestershire sauce
½ to 1½ teaspoons hot red pepper sauce, to taste
1½ teaspoons salt

2 to 3 tablespoons coarsely cracked black pepper
Zest and juice of 1 lemon
3 pounds large, uncooked shrimp (15 to 16 shrimp per pound), peeled and deveined
French, italian, or artesian breads

Preheat oven to 400 degrees. Put butter in large microwave-safe bowl and heat until melted. If using olive oil instead of butter, place it in large bowl for mixing. To butter or olive oil, add onion, garlic, rosemary, Worcestershire, hot red pepper sauce, salt, pepper, lemon juice, and zest, stirring to mix thoroughly. Check for spiciness and adjust seasoning, if necessary. Place shrimp in baking dish and stir butter spice mixture over them. Bake about 10 to 12 minutes, turn shrimp, and bake 10 to 12 minutes longer, until shrimp are tender and just cooked. Warm bread and cut into large cubes. Serve with shrimp to dip into sauce. Yield: 12 to 15 appetizer servings

Notes

....

....

....

....

Tuna Appetizers

Serve these spreads with assorted crackers, breads, or various fresh vegetables.

Zesty Tuna Ball

1 (8 ounce) package cream cheese, softened
1 (12 ounce) can tuna, packed in water, slightly drained
1 medium onion, finely chopped

1½ to 2 teaspoons hot red pepper sauce, to taste
1½ teaspoons fresh dill, chopped
1½ cups finely chopped walnuts or cashews, divided

Thoroughly combine cream cheese, tuna, onion, hot pepper sauce, dill, and 1 cup chopped nuts in bowl. Refrigerate for about 2 hours. Place remaining

½ cup nuts into shallow dish. Mold cold tuna mixture in ball and roll ball in nuts. Refrigerate 30 minutes before serving.

Tuna with Beans

1 (12 ounce) can tuna, packed in water, drained
2 tablespoons olive oil
1 (15 ounce) can cannellini beans, drained and rinsed

1 medium onion, finely chopped
2 tablespoons fresh parsley, chopped
1 teaspoon lemon juice
Salt and freshly ground black pepper to taste

Place tuna and oil into food processor bowl. Add beans, onion, parsley, and lemon juice. Pulse ingredients until well mixed and smooth. Taste tuna mixture and season with salt and pepper to taste. Transfer to serving dish. Refrigerate for at least 2 hours before serving.

Tomato Salad Bites

These miniature salad appetizers are delicious and easy to prepare and serve.

Tomato Cheese Bites

30 cherry tomatoes
8 ounces goat cheese
2 tablespoons fresh basil leaves,
   finely chopped

¼ cup olive oil
3 tablespoons balsamic vinegar
Salt and pepper to taste

Wash and wipe dry tomatoes. Cut off a small slice on the bottom of each tomato so that they will stand up on a serving platter. Cut off tops, core, and scoop the pulp out of tomatoes and discard pulp. Combine cheese and basil.

Fill each tomato with cheese mixture with a spoon or scoop.* Stir together oil and vinegar and drizzle on top of tomatoes. Refrigerate until serving; serve at room temperature for best taste. Yield: 15 appetizer servings

*NOTE: If desired, transfer to a pastry bag fitted with a star tip. Pipe the cheese mixture into center of each tomato.

Notes

....

....

....

....

Tomato Shrimp and Cheese Bites

30 cherry tomatoes
1½ cups cooked shrimp, finely chopped
1 (8 ounce) package cream cheese,
  softened

2 tablespoons fresh dill, finely chopped
¼ cup olive oil
3 tablespoons balsamic vinegar
Salt and pepper to taste

Wash and wipe dry tomatoes. Cut off a small slice on the bottom of each tomato, so that they will stand up on a serving platter. Cut off tops, core, and scoop the pulp out of tomatoes and discard pulp. Combine shrimp, cream cheese, and dill; insert about 1 teaspoon of mixture into center of each tomato. Stir together oil and vinegar and drizzle and on top of tomatoes. Refrigerate until serving; serve at room temperature for best taste. Yield: 15 appetizer servings

Notes

....
....
....
....
....
....
....

The Festive Feast: Main Dishes

Whether your holiday get-together is a formal affair or just good friends getting together to celebrate the season, advance planning is the key to success! Begin with a guest list that will fit comfortably in your home. Will your party be a family affair with kids or adults only? Plan the date, and send out an invitation—snail mail, e-vite, or text—whatever suits your style. Next, plan the menu. Will you be preparing everything yourself, or will you ask your guests to bring a prepared appetizer or dessert? Other than your normal Christmas decorations, will you add anything to your table or serving area to make the mood more festive? And finally, what activities or games will you play during the party? (See the last section of this book for some fun ideas.)

But give me holly, bold and jolly,
Honest, prickly, shining holly;
Pluck me holly leaf and berry
For the days when I make merry.

CHRISTINA GEORGINA ROSSETTI

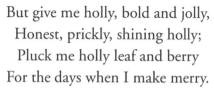

Honey-Glazed Stuffed Ham Rolls

12 (⅛-inch thick) slices fully cooked ham
2 cups grated apple
1 cup chopped cranberries
1 cup dry bread crumbs
¼ teaspoon salt
¼ teaspoon pepper
2 teaspoons dry mustard

1 teaspoon ground ginger
4 tablespoons melted butter
1 cup honey
½ cup brown sugar, packed
¼ cup apple cider or water
12 whole cloves
1 (4 inch) cinnamon stick, broken in half

Lay ham slices out on piece of foil or waxed paper. Thoroughly combine apples, cranberries, bread crumbs, salt, pepper, dry mustard, ginger, and melted butter. Divide mixture evenly on each of the ham slices. Roll up each ham slice and secure with toothpicks or butcher's string. Arrange ham rolls in lightly greased or foil-lined roasting pan or baking dish. In saucepan over medium heat, cook honey, brown sugar, apple cider, cloves, and cinnamon stick until mixture is well combined but not boiling. Remove pan from heat. Spoon glaze over ham rolls. Bake at 400 degrees for 30 to 45 minutes, basting frequently with glaze. When done, remove from oven and set aside, letting ham rest for 5 minutes. Transfer to warm serving platter. Yield: 12 servings

Notes

Roast Game Hens with Wild Rice Stuffing

1½ cups wild or brown rice
¼ cup finely chopped onion
¼ cup unsalted butter
1 clove garlic, finely minced
½ pound mushrooms,
    cleaned and sliced
2 tablespoons fresh parsley,
    finely chopped

½ teaspoon poultry seasoning
Salt and pepper
6 (1 pound) whole cornish game hens
6 tablespoons unsalted butter, softened
¾ cup hot chicken broth or stock
1 teaspoon cornstarch, dissolved in
    ⅛ cup water

Preheat oven to 450 degrees. Spray roasting pan with nonstick spray; set aside.
To make stuffing, cook rice according to package directions. In skillet, cook
chopped onion in butter for 5 minutes, stirring constantly. Add garlic and

mushrooms and cook 5 minutes longer, stirring occasionally. Add cooked rice, parsley, and poultry seasoning. Taste and add salt and pepper to taste. Divide rice stuffing evenly between game hens. Tie legs of each hen together with a piece of butcher's string. Place hens in prepared pan breast side up. Rub each with 1 tablespoon butter. Roast hens for 15 minutes or until they begin to brown. Lower heat to 350 degrees and roast about 30 to 40 minutes longer or until internal temperature reaches 165 degrees when tested in breast meat on meat thermometer. When done, leg joints should easily move. Transfer hens to warmed serving platters; set aside to keep them warm.

Whisk hot chicken broth into juices in roasting pan, scraping the brown bits from bottom of pan. Add in cornstarch water, whisking constantly to prevent lumps; cook until sauce is clear. Strain sauce through a fine sieve into gravy boat. Serve. Yield: 6 servings

Stuffed Flank Steak

1 (10 ounce) package frozen
  chopped spinach
¾ cup diced celery
1 small onion, diced
5 tablespoons olive oil
½ teaspoon dried savory

¾ teaspoon salt
⅛ teaspoon pepper
4 cups bread cubes
1 (2 to 3 pound) flank steak
3 tablespoons oil

Cook spinach per package directions. Transfer spinach to fine-meshed sieve over a bowl. Press out liquid, catching any remaining cooking liquid in bowl. Let spinach drain a few minutes longer. Transfer spinach to chopping board and chop it finely; set aside. In skillet over medium heat cook celery and onion in olive oil until softened. Stir in savory, salt, pepper, and spinach. Place bread cubes in large bowl. Mix in spinach mixture. Add some of reserved liquid to lightly moisten bread, if necessary. Lay flank steak out on piece of foil or waxed paper. Spread stuffing mix over flank steak. Beginning at narrow end, roll steak like a jelly roll. Secure stuffed steak with butcher's string in two or three places. Preheat oven to 350 degrees. Heat oil in large ovenproof skillet. Brown steak on all sides in oil. Lift steak with tongs; place small roasting rack under steak. Place tight-fitting lid on skillet; place pan in oven. Bake for 1 to 1½ hours. Remove steak to warm serving platter. If desired, make gravy with drippings. To serve steak, carve at end across the grain so that each serving is a round slice with stuffing in the center. Yield: 6 to 8 servings

Skewered Shrimp, Pineapple, and Onions with Rice

24 large shrimp, peeled and deveined
18 to 20 pineapple chunks cut into
   1-inch cubes
18 to 20 pearl onions
2 to 3 green bell peppers cut into
   1½-inch pieces

¼ cup soy sauce
¼ cup orange juice
1 slice fresh ginger cut ¼ inch thick
1 tablespoon honey
3 cups cooked rice

Alternating shrimp, pineapple chunks, pearl onions, and pieces of bell pepper, thread ingredients onto 12-inch skewers; set aside. In saucepan over medium heat, combine soy sauce, orange juice, ginger slice, and honey, stirring constantly. Bring to simmer; still stirring, cook until glaze has slightly thickened. Remove from heat to cool; discard ginger. Preheat oven broiler. Position oven rack about 5 inches below broiler element or flame. Spray a broiler pan with nonstick cooking spray. Brush shrimp with glaze. Place skewers on prepared broiler pan and place under broiler and cook for about 10 minutes. While shrimp are cooking, brush with glaze occasionally, and turn several times until shrimp are cooked and curled and pineapple, onions, and pepper pieces are lightly browned. Serve over hot rice. Yield: 6 servings

Lorraine's Chicken à la King

This party classic can be made with any type of poultry.

1 cup unsalted butter or olive oil
½ cup diced green bell pepper
½ cup diced red bell pepper
¼ pound fresh mushrooms, cleaned,
   trimmed, and thinly sliced*
1 cup flour
1 teaspoon salt
¼ teaspoon pepper, or to taste

2 cups chicken stock or broth
2 cups milk, warmed
1 teaspoon dried tarragon
4 to 5 cups cooked chicken,
   diced into bite-sized pieces
Prebaked pastry shells, dinner rolls,
   or biscuits

Heat butter or oil over medium-low heat in large saucepan, and sauté green and red bell peppers with mushrooms. Stir in flour, salt, and pepper, cooking until flour is well blended and mixture begins to bubble. On low heat, slowly stir in stock, milk, and tarragon, stirring constantly. Let mixture boil for 1 minute. Add cooked chicken and heat through. Transfer chicken and sauce mixture to slow cooker set on low and cover it to keep hot. Serve in prepared pastry shells or on top of freshly baked biscuits. Yield: 10 to 12 servings

NOTE: 2 (2.5 ounce) jars mushrooms, drained, may be used instead.

Notes

Cranberry Pork Roast

Make this tender roast in your 6-quart slow cooker.

2 tablespoons vegetable oil
1 (4 pound) boneless pork loin
1 (16 ounce) can whole-berry cranberry
   sauce or homemade equivalent
¾ cup honey
½ to ¾ cup cranberry juice cocktail,
   any variety

1 teaspoon ground mustard
1 teaspoon black pepper
¼ teaspoon ground cloves
¼ cup cold water
¼ cup cornstarch
Salt to taste

In dutch oven, heat oil over medium-high heat. Brown pork loin on all sides.

Transfer roast to slow cooker. In bowl, combine cranberry sauce, honey,

   cranberry juice cocktail, mustard, black pepper, and cloves; pour mixture over roast. Cover and cook roast on a low temperature setting for 6 to 8 hours or until meat reaches an internal temperature of 160 degrees. Remove roast from slow cooker; place on warm platter and cover to keep warm. In saucepan, whisk together cold water and cornstarch, blending to ensure it is free of lumps. Stir in cooking juices from slow cooker. Bring mixture to a boil, stirring constantly. Boil and stir for 2 minutes or until sauce is thickened. Transfer sauce to heated gravy boat or serving dish; serve with roast. Yield: 10 to 12 servings

Notes

Mushroomed Scallops with Mashed Potatoes

2 pounds potatoes
8 large scallops
½ pound fresh button mushrooms,
    cleaned, trimmed, and thinly sliced
2½ cups water
1½ cups fish stock or clam juice
2 lemon slices

2 bay leaves
4 tablespoons unsalted butter
4 tablespoons flour
Salt and pepper to taste
2 egg yolks, well beaten
4 tablespoons heavy cream
4 tablespoons unsalted butter, melted

Peel and quarter potatoes. Place potatoes in pot and bring to a boil. Cook until potatoes are fork tender. Mash and season potatoes; keep warm. Meanwhile, wash scallops quickly under cold running water; dry with toweling. Cut each scallop into 4 to 6 slices. Place scallops and mushrooms in large saucepan with water, stock, lemon slices, and bay leaves. Bring to a boil; then reduce heat, cover, and simmer for 15 to 20 minutes. Strain through a colander, reserving 2½ cups of the cooking liquid. Discard lemon slices and bay leaves. Keep scallops and mushrooms warm. In large saucepan over low heat, melt butter. Whisk in flour, cooking for a few minutes. Gradually add reserved liquid, whisking continuously until sauce is smooth. Bring to a boil; simmer 3 to 4 minutes. Stir in scallops and mushrooms; taste for seasoning. Reheat on low. Combine egg yolks and cream. Remove scallop mixture from heat and stir in the yolk mixture. Spray large shallow baking dish with nonstick cooking spray. Pipe or spoon mashed potatoes along outer edges of dish. Brush mashed potatoes with melted butter. Spoon scallop mixture into center of dish. Broil for 2 to 3 minutes until potatoes are golden. Serve. Yield: 6 to 8 servings

Peppered Beef Fillet

¾ cup unsalted butter, softened
1 tablespoon lemon juice
2 teaspoons dried tarragon or rosemary
1 (3 to 4 pound) fillet of beef, trimmed

3½ tablespoons extra-virgin olive oil
¼ to ½ cup coarsely ground black or
  mixed peppercorns
Salt to taste

Combine butter, lemon juice, and tarragon or rosemary in bowl until
thoroughly combined. Place mixture on piece of foil and shape into a 4-inch-
long log. Refrigerate. Bring fillet to room temperature; wipe all sides with
toweling. Preheat oven to 450 degrees. Line roasting pan with foil and insert
roasting rack; set aside. Brush fillet lightly with olive oil. Evenly distribute
peppercorns in a flat shallow dish large enough to hold fillet. Place fillet
on peppercorns, pressing down slightly so that peppercorns stick to sides;

roll fillet to cover all sides. Place meat on rack in roasting pan. Insert meat thermometer into thickest part of fillet. Place pan in oven and immediately reduce oven temperature to 400 degrees. Roast fillet until it reaches desired stage of doneness (i.e., rare, medium). The roasting time will depend on thickness of fillet and temperature of meat before it was placed in oven; start checking temperature after 30 minutes. When fillet is removed from oven, internal temperature will rise a bit. Remove fillet from oven, cover with foil, and let it rest for 10 minutes before slicing. Cut fillet into 6 to 8 slices. Just before serving, cut herb butter into 12 pieces and serve with fillet. Yield: 6 to 8 servings

Roast Lamb Crown

4 tablespoons unsalted butter
¼ cup onion, finely chopped
2 cups mushrooms, cleaned and
   finely chopped
1½ teaspoons dried rosemary
½ teaspoon dried thyme
2 cups fresh bread cubes

½ cup hazelnuts, chopped
½ cup chicken stock or broth
Salt and pepper to taste
2 lamb rib roasts, 12 to 16 ribs total
1 tablespoon olive oil
Salt and pepper to taste

Preheat oven to 450 degrees. Line roasting pan with foil; set aside. Melt butter in large skillet over low heat. Stir in onion and mushrooms and cook until tender, about 5 to 7 minutes. Transfer onion and mushrooms to large mixing bowl. Stir in rosemary, thyme, bread cubes, hazelnuts, and stock. Check seasoning and add salt and pepper to taste; set aside. Rub lamb with olive oil and sprinkle with salt and pepper. Cover ends of bones with foil so they do not burn. Place lamb in pan, fill center of roast with stuffing mixture, and place pan in oven. Immediately reduce heat to 350 degrees. Roast lamb until it reaches desired stage of doneness (i.e., 20 minutes per pound for medium rare, 30 minutes per pound for medium). When removed from oven, internal temperature will rise a bit. Remove roasting pan from oven, remove foil from bone ends, and allow meat to rest for 10 minutes. Transfer to warm serving platter. Yield: approximately 6 to 8 servings

Spinach Cheese Tortellini

PASTA:
4 cups flour
1 teaspoon salt
4 large eggs
2 teaspoons water
2 teaspoons olive oil

FILLING:
½ pound fresh spinach, trimmed, washed
1 cup ricotta cheese
1 cup grated parmesan cheese
1 egg yolk
Salt and pepper to taste

PASTA: Place flour and salt in bowl; make a well in center. Add eggs, water, and olive oil. Beat with a fork, incorporating flour. When all flour is moistened, press into rough ball. On lightly floured board, knead dough vigorously 10 to 15 minutes until smooth and firm. If dough is sticky, add 1 tablespoon flour; if dough is dry, add a few drops warm water. Cover with damp towel for 30 minutes to rest. FILLING: Cook spinach in small amount of water 3 to 5 minutes. Drain, squeeze dry; chop finely. Combine with cheeses, egg yolk, salt, and pepper; set aside. PASTA: Shape dough into a flat circle. Roll on lightly floured board, as for pie crust; move rolling pin from center outward. Give dough a quarter turn after each roll. Check occasionally that dough isn't sticking to board; add flour if necessary. When dough is ⅛-inch thick, roll and stretch until very thin. Using 2-inch biscuit cutter, cut circles from dough. Keep circles covered with damp towel. Place ½ teaspoon filling in center of each circle. Fold in half so edges almost meet; pinch edges together. Fold small ends of the half circles so they meet, crossing to form a bundle. Pinch the overlap together. Place assembled tortellini on towel, not touching each other. When done, leave tortellini to dry 1 hour or overnight. Bring salted water to boil. Add no more than 10 or 12 tortellini at once; cook for 5 to 7 minutes. Remove to colander. Serve with melted butter, grated parmesan cheese, or light tomato sauce. Yield: 100 tortellini

Tourtière

1 pound lean ground pork
½ pound ground veal or lean ground beef
6 slices bacon, cut up
½ cup onion, finely chopped
½ cup celery, finely chopped
2 cloves garlic, finely minced
2 teaspoons dried sage
¼ teaspoon salt
⅛ teaspoon pepper
1¼ cups water, divided

2 tablespoons cornstarch or
    all-purpose flour
2 cups flour
1 teaspoon salt
6 tablespoons cold unsalted butter,
    cut into small pieces
6 tablespoons cold shortening,
    cut into small pieces
5 to 6 tablespoons ice water

In large pot brown pork, veal, and bacon. Drain off fat. Add onion, celery,
    garlic, sage, ¼ teaspoon salt, and pepper, stirring well. Stir in 1 cup water;

bring mixture to a boil. Reduce heat to low. Simmer covered until onion is tender, stirring frequently. Whisk together remaining water and cornstarch until smooth. Stir into meat mixture, cooking until mixture is thick and bubbly. Cook and stir 2 minutes longer. Remove from heat; let mixture cool slightly.

Combine flour and salt in bowl. With pastry knife cut in butter and shortening until mixture resembles coarse crumbs. Add ice water a tablespoon at a time; add just enough so dough just holds together. Divide dough in half, forming each half into slightly flattened balls. Wrap in plastic wrap; refrigerate 1 hour. On lightly floured board, roll out one-half of dough into a 10-inch circle. Fit into 9-inch pie plate. Fill with meat mixture. Roll out remaining dough into a 10-inch circle; place on top of pie. Preheat oven to 400 degrees. Crimp edges of pastry. Prick top crust to allow steam to escape while baking. Bake 20 to 25 minutes or until golden brown. Cool at least 15 minutes before serving. Tourtière can also be served cold. Yield: 6 servings

Leg of Lamb with Potatoes, Onions, and Gravy

6 large potatoes, peeled, thinly sliced
2 medium onions, thinly sliced
Salt and pepper to taste
5 tablespoons butter
1 teaspoon ground ginger
1 teaspoon dried rosemary
1 teaspoon salt

¼ teaspoon pepper
1 (5 to 6 pound) leg of lamb
1 cup apple cider
⅔ cup honey
1 tablespoon quick-blending flour
   or cornstarch
1 tablespoon water

Preheat oven to 325 degrees. Place one-third of sliced potatoes in well-greased 2-quart baking dish. Place one-half of sliced onions on top of potatoes. Sprinkle with salt and pepper and dot with 1 tablespoon butter. Keep layering potato slices, onion slices, salt, pepper, and butter, ending with a layer of potatoes and remaining butter. Bake covered for 1 hour; uncovered for 30 minutes. If vegetables are done before lamb, remove them from oven; cover and keep warm.

Line roasting pan with foil. In small bowl combine ginger, rosemary, salt, and pepper. Rub lamb with spice mixture. Place lamb fat side up in roasting pan. Roast lamb uncovered for 1 hour. Combine cider and honey. Pour cider mixture over lamb. Basting occasionally, roast lamb for 1½ hours longer or until meat reaches an internal temperature of 160 degrees on meat thermometer. Transfer lamb to warm serving platter and keep warm. Drain fat from drippings. Measure 1 cup pan drippings and place in saucepan or back into roasting pan. Whisk flour and water together and add to drippings. Whisk and cook until thickened. Stir and cook 2 minutes longer. Transfer sauce to heated gravy boat. Yield: 6 servings

Rabbit or Chicken Casserole

This recipe was created for use with rabbit.
Chicken can be substituted if you prefer.

⅓ cup oil or butter
1 (2 to 3 pound) rabbit or chicken, cut up
1¼ cups onion, coarsely chopped
1 cup carrot, peeled and coarsely chopped
⅓ cup walnuts, coarsely chopped
¼ pound fresh mushrooms, cleaned,
    trimmed, and thinly sliced*

2 tablespoons quick-blending
    or all-purpose flour
1 teaspoon salt
¼ teaspoon pepper
1 cup apple juice or cider
Noodles or rice for serving

In large skillet, heat oil. Cook rabbit or chicken pieces on all sides until nicely browned. Transfer meat to 3-quart casserole; reserve drippings in skillet.

Add onion, carrot, and walnuts to drippings. Cook until vegetables are tender but not brown. Stir in mushrooms, cooking them about 2 minutes. Spoon vegetables, walnuts, and mushrooms over meat in casserole dish; reserve drippings in skillet. Whisk flour, salt, and pepper into drippings. Add apple juice or cider all at once, whisking and cooking until mixture is thickened and bubbly. Cook and stir 1 minute longer. Pour gravy over ingredients in casserole. Bake covered at 350 degrees for 1 hour or until meat is done. Serve over noodles or rice. Yield: 4 to 6 servings

NOTE: 2 (2.5 ounce) jars mushrooms, drained, may be used instead.

Honey Lemon Duck

½ cup honey
½ cup pomegranate juice
½ cup lemon juice
1 (5 to 6 pound) duck
½ lemon, cut into wedges

1 small apple, quartered
3 slices fresh ginger, cut ¼-inch thick
1 small onion, sliced
1 teaspoon salt

Preheat oven to 350 degrees. Spray roasting pan with nonstick spray. Insert roasting rack in pan. Add 2 inches of water in bottom of pan; set aside. In bowl, combine honey with pomegranate and lemon juices, stirring until sauce is smooth and thoroughly combined; set aside. Wipe duck with toweling. Place lemon, apple, ginger, and onion in cavity of duck. Tie legs together with a piece of butcher's string to close cavity. Sprinkle duck with salt and place duck on rack in roasting pan. Put duck in oven. Roast duck for 2 hours, brushing with honey sauce every 10 to 15 minutes. Roast until bird is rich brown and juices run clear when thigh is pierced with tip of a sharp knife. Let duck rest on warm platter before slicing. Serve with remaining sauce if desired. Roasted potatoes and steamed broccoli complement this duck recipe. Yield: 6 to 8 servings

Notes

Beef Rib Roast with Gravy and Horseradish Sauce

2 cloves garlic, crushed
Salt and pepper
1 (6 to 8 pound) standing rib roast
4 tablespoons fat from drippings
4 tablespoons flour
2 cups beef drippings

½ cup heavy cream
Pinch salt
Pinch sugar
Pinch freshly ground black pepper
2 tablespoons grated horseradish
1 teaspoon lemon juice

Preheat oven to 325 degrees. Spray large roasting pan with nonstick cooking spray. Mix garlic with salt and pepper. Rub mixture over roast. Place roast in prepared pan. Roast beef uncovered until meat reaches an internal temperature of desired doneness on meat thermometer (140 degrees for rare, 160 degrees for medium, 170 degrees for well done). Transfer roast to warm serving platter and allow it to rest for 10 minutes.

To make gravy, drain fat from drippings. Measure 2 cups drippings; set aside. Measure 4 tablespoons of fat and return them to roasting pan. Whisk flour into fat and scrape up any browned particles stuck inside bottom of pan. Cook flour until it is lightly browned. Add drippings and cook gravy, whisking until gravy is thickened. Stir and cook 2 minutes longer. Transfer gravy to warm gravy boat.

HORSERADISH SAUCE: Whip cream until soft peaks form. Add salt, sugar, and pepper. Fold in horseradish and lemon juice. Serve with roast beef and/or roasted vegetables.

All the Trimmings: Sides

Sides are wonderful elements of every meal, and they can make or break your feast. When planning your menu for any party, consider the colors of the foods in the side dishes you plan to serve, and be sure to have a variety of pleasing hues that will look good on a plate. Along with color, you may want to have sides with a variety of pleasing palate textures. And if you know your guests well enough, you may want to accommodate picky eaters by choosing sides that you know everyone will enjoy.

Whatever you do, don't wait until the last minute to do this part of your menu planning! In fact, you may want to choose your sides first and then pick a main dish that complements the unique flavors that you have chosen. Thinking outside of the box this way may just lead you to your new favorite Christmas menu!

O star of wonder, star of night,
Star with royal beauty bright,
Westward leading, still proceeding,
Guide us to Thy perfect light.

JOHN HENRY HOPKINS

Carrot Quiche

1 large egg
1 tablespoon lemon juice
2 cups flour
¼ teaspoon salt
8 tablespoons butter
1 well-beaten egg yolk, for glazing
5 carrots, peeled and grated
4 tablespoons butter, melted
1 teaspoon salt

⅛ teaspoon dried marjoram
2 tablespoons fresh parsley, finely chopped
1 teaspoon dijon-style mustard
4 tablespoons grated parmesan cheese
3 egg yolks
2 large eggs
⅔ cup heavy cream
⅛ teaspoon ground nutmeg

Beat egg and lemon juice together; set aside. Sift flour and salt into bowl. Add butter and beaten egg mixture. Blend mixture together until butter is fully incorporated and dough is stiff. Add 2 tablespoons cold water, if necessary, to hold dough together. Form into ball, wrap in plastic wrap, and refrigerate for 1 hour. Preheat oven to 425 degrees. On a lightly floured board, roll dough to fit a 9-inch pie pan. Line dough with foil or parchment paper and fill it with pie weights. Bake 15 minutes; remove foil and pie weights. Brush yolk over crust; bake 3 minutes longer; let cool. Reduce oven temperature to 350 degrees. Bring saucepan of water to a boil, blanch carrots for 1 minute; drain. Mix carrots, melted butter, salt, marjoram, and parsley; set aside. Brush crust with mustard. Spread carrot filling evenly in crust; top with parmesan cheese. Beat together egg yolks, eggs, cream, and nutmeg; pour this mixture over carrots. Bake for 35 minutes or until knife inserted in center comes out clean.

Baked Sweet Onions or Beets

4 to 5 large sweet white or red onions*
2 tablespoons olive oil
⅓ cup vegetable, chicken, or beef stock
 or broth
1½ teaspoons balsamic vinegar

¾ teaspoon dried rosemary
¾ teaspoon dried thyme
½ teaspoon salt
¼ teaspoon pepper

Preheat oven to 350 degrees. Line large shallow baking dish with foil, extending foil on all sides so that edges can be folded over to cover onions loosely and meet in center to form a packet. Lightly grease foil with nonstick cooking spray. (Instead of using foil, use a baking dish with lid and spray both with nonstick cooking spray.) Peel onions and trim root and stem ends.

Cut each onion in half. Place onions, cut side up, in baking dish. Combine olive oil, stock, and vinegar in bowl. Evenly spoon mixture over each onion. Sprinkle herbs, salt, and pepper over onions. Bring ends of foil together and fold to close. Bake onions for 1 hour. Open foil (or remove lid) to expose onions. Bake until onions are very tender, about 30 minutes longer. Yield: 8 to 10 servings

NOTE: Instead of onions, substitute 3 pounds fresh beets. Wearing plastic gloves or bags on your hands, peel and remove tops and root ends with sharp knife. Rinse in cold water. Continue as per above recipe.

Winter Salad

2 cups fresh broccoli florets
4 carrots, peeled and thinly sliced
4 romaine hearts, cleaned, trimmed,
  and torn into bite-sized pieces
2 cups mixed greens or fresh spinach,
  cleaned and trimmed
4 pears, washed, cored, and thinly sliced
3 tablespoons balsamic, herbal,
  or fruit vinegar
1 cup plain yogurt

¼ cup mayonnaise
1 tablespoon honey
2 tablespoons green onions, finely sliced
¾ teaspoon salt
½ teaspoon freshly ground black pepper
4 to 6 ounces bleu cheese, crumbled
¾ cup pomegranate seeds
½ to ¾ cup coarsely chopped walnuts
  or pecans, optional

Bring 1 inch of water to a boil in saucepan. Add broccoli florets and carrots
and cook over medium heat for 3 minutes. Drain well. In large bowl toss

romaine, mixed greens, broccoli florets, carrot slices, and pear slices. The salad can be made ahead of time up to this point. Cover with damp tea towel and refrigerate until serving. Combine vinegar, yogurt, mayonnaise, honey, green onions, salt, and pepper in bowl or jar with a tight-fitting lid, blending well, to make salad dressing. Add dressing to salad and toss lightly. Sprinkle bleu cheese, pomegranate seeds, and nuts over top of salad before serving. Yield: 8 to 10 servings

Notes

Leek Ricotta Cheese Tart

This tart makes a wonderful side dish or vegetarian main dish.

1½ cups flour
½ teaspoon salt
⅛ teaspoon sugar
6 tablespoons cold unsalted butter,
    cut into small pieces
2 tablespoons cold shortening
3 to 4 tablespoons ice water
4 tablespoons unsalted butter
1½ cups coarsely chopped leeks,
    white parts only

1½ cups ricotta cheese
¼ cup grated parmesan cheese
3 large eggs, well beaten
2 teaspoons green onions, finely sliced
1 teaspoon dried parsley
½ teaspoon dried thyme
½ teaspoon salt
⅛ teaspoon freshly ground black pepper

Sift together flour, salt, and sugar in large bowl. With pastry knife, cut in 6 tablespoons butter and shortening until mixture resembles coarse crumbs. Add enough ice water so dough just holds together. Form dough into ball and flatten it slightly. Wrap in plastic wrap and refrigerate for 1 hour. Meanwhile, prepare filling. In a skillet, heat 4 tablespoons butter over low heat. Add leeks; cook until leeks are soft and golden, stirring frequently. In a bowl beat together ricotta, parmesan cheese, eggs, onions, parsley, thyme, salt, and pepper. Stir leeks into cheese mixture; set aside. On a lightly floured board and with a lightly floured rolling pin, roll out dough to a ⅛-inch thickness. Fit dough into 9-inch deep dish pie plate, pressing dough into bottom and sides of plate. Cover with plastic wrap and refrigerate for 30 minutes. Preheat oven to 375 degrees. Spoon leek mixture into tart shell. Bake for 30 minutes or until filling is set and top is golden brown.

Yield: 6 to 8 servings

Candace's Green Beans, Bell Pepper, and Olive Sauté

This flavorful dish cooks up quickly, so have all ingredients prepped before starting dish on stove. Fresh asparagus or broccoli spears may be substituted for fresh green beans, if desired.

1 tablespoon lemon juice, fresh if available
½ teaspoon dijon-style mustard
Salt and freshly ground black pepper, to taste
2 cloves garlic, minced
5 kalamata olives, pitted and chopped*
1 tablespoon olive oil

1 pound fresh green beans, cleaned and trimmed
½ cup red bell pepper, seeded, roughly chopped
½ cup water or stock
2 tablespoons fresh parsley, chopped

Whisk together lemon juice, mustard, salt, and pepper; set aside. In large skillet, over medium heat, sauté garlic and olives in olive oil for 30 seconds. Add green beans, bell pepper, and water; cover and cook just until green beans are tender, about 3 to 5 minutes. Uncover and stir in lemon-mustard seasoning. Transfer to heated serving dish, if desired. Garnish with fresh parsley; if using dried parsley, add it to dish with lemon-mustard seasoning. Serve hot. Yield: 6 to 8 servings

Notes

Baked Spinach

Dry bread crumbs
2 (10 ounce) packages frozen chopped
  spinach*
1 tablespoon butter
2 tablespoons water
Pinch of salt
1 whole clove garlic, peeled
2 tablespoons butter

1 heaping tablespoon flour
4 large eggs, separated
Pinch of salt
3 large hard-cooked eggs,
  cooled and sliced
2 tablespoons butter, softened
¼ teaspoon ground nutmeg
⅛ teaspoon freshly ground black pepper

Preheat oven to 350 degrees. Butter large baking dish; lightly sprinkle bottom
and sides with bread crumbs. Break up frozen spinach. Place in saucepan with
1 tablespoon butter, water, salt, and garlic. Cook on low heat, breaking up
spinach until water has completely boiled away. Remove from heat. Discard

garlic; pour spinach into fine-meshed sieve. Press out remaining liquid; let spinach drain a few minutes longer. Transfer spinach to chopping board and chop finely. Transfer spinach to mixing bowl. Melt 2 tablespoons butter in saucepan over low heat. Whisk in flour, cooking for 2 to 3 minutes to make a roux. Whisk roux and egg yolks into spinach. Beat egg whites with salt until stiff peaks form. Stir in 1 tablespoon spinach mixture; gently fold in remaining spinach mixture. Spoon a layer of spinach in prepared baking dish. Top with layer of sliced hard-cooked eggs. Continue layering spinach and egg slices until both are used, ending with a layer of spinach. Combine softened butter, nutmeg, and pepper; dot over top of spinach. Bake 30 minutes until spinach puffs and is lightly browned on top.

NOTE: Use 3 pounds cleaned, trimmed fresh spinach or swiss chard leaves instead of frozen spinach. Prepare and bake as above.

Potato Roses

These roses are an attractive presentation of potatoes and are not as difficult to create as you may think. The roses can be made up to 1 day before serving.

4 pounds baking potatoes
¼ cup butter, softened
2 tablespoons minced onion
1½ teaspoons salt
⅛ teaspoon freshly ground black pepper
1 tablespoon fresh parsley, minced

2 tablespoons grated parmesan or
   romano cheese
1 large egg
Paprika
½ cup butter, melted

Peel potatoes; cut in halves. Cook in boiling water until tender; drain. Mash potatoes slightly. Place potatoes in large mixing bowl; beat until light and fluffy. Add softened butter, onion, salt, pepper, parsley, cheese, and egg. Whip until potatoes are well mixed. Cool. Using a scoop, or your hands moistened with cold water, shape potatoes into ¾-cup-sized balls. Place potato balls on lightly greased baking sheet; flatten bottoms of balls slightly. To form roses, dip your forefinger in cold water and use it to make an indentation in the center of each potato ball. Swirl your finger clockwise to make a spiral outward. If desired, cover with plastic wrap and refrigerate overnight. Bring potato roses up to room temperature before baking. Preheat oven to 450 degrees. Sprinkle each potato rose lightly with paprika and drizzle melted butter evenly over each. Bake for 8 minutes. Let rest before transferring to warm serving platter. Yield: 10 servings

Orange Rice Dressing or Stuffing

*This recipe makes enough to stuff a 12- to 14-pound turkey or goose.
In this offering, it is partially baked in a casserole dish and served as a side dish.
This recipe can be made with white rice or brown rice or with a mixture of white,
brown, and wild rice. It is good with fowl, fish, and meat.*

1 cup butter or olive oil
1 cup onions, chopped
4 cups celery, chopped
4 cups water
2 cups orange juice
4 tablespoons orange zest

1 tablespoon salt
1 teaspoon poultry seasoning
4 cups rice, uncooked
½ cup fresh parsley, chopped
Freshly ground black pepper to taste

Preheat oven to 325 degrees. Heat butter in large saucepan over low heat.

Add onions and celery and cook 8 to 10 minutes until onions are soft. Stir in water, orange juice, orange zest, salt, poultry seasoning, and rice. Bring liquid to a boil over high heat, stirring occasionally. Reduce heat to low; cover and cook for about 15 minutes. Add parsley and pepper, stirring to blend well.* Transfer to buttered casserole dish; cover. Bake until rice is done, 15 minutes or longer, depending on type of rice being used. Yield: 10 to 12 servings

*NOTE: At this point the Orange Rice can be used for stuffing. Bake per recipe for your entrée meat.

Herbed Beans and Broccoli

This colorful dish goes together quickly after dried beans have cooked. Using a variety of beans gives a multitude of colors and tastes. We have used cannellini, scarlet runner, and Christmas lima beans in this dish with tasty results.

1 cup dried large beans*
1 pound broccoli florets, trimmed
½ cup butter, melted or extra-virgin
   olive oil

½ teaspoon dried thyme
Salt and freshly ground pepper to taste

In large saucepan, cover dried beans with cold water, cover, and let soak at least 8 hours or overnight. Drain and rinse beans. Place soaked beans in large pot. Add water to twice the depth of beans. Bring to a boil over high heat and cook for 10 minutes. Stir. Reduce heat to low and simmer beans until tender. Drain in colander. In large saucepan bring 2 inches of water to a boil over high heat. Insert steamer basket and steam broccoli florets until crisp-tender, about 5 to 7 minutes. Drain broccoli. Combine beans and broccoli in casserole dish with lid. Combine melted butter or olive oil, thyme, salt, and pepper in small bowl. Pour mixture over beans and broccoli, tossing to coat. This dish may be served hot, warm, or cold. Yield: 6 servings

NOTE: In a hurry? Substitute 3 cups precooked beans. If using canned beans, rinse well before using.

Millet Vegetable Casserole

Serve this delicious casserole as a side dish or as a vegetarian main dish.

4 tablespoons olive oil, divided
2 large onions, chopped, divided
1 cup millet
3 cups vegetable stock, chicken stock,
   or water, divided
¾ pound butternut squash, peeled,
   cut into 1-inch cubes
¾ pound sweet potatoes, peeled,
   cut into 1-inch cubes

1¼ teaspoons hungarian hot or
   sweet paprika
½ teaspoon cumin
½ teaspoon ground ginger
½ teaspoon ground cinnamon
Salt to taste

Heat 2 tablespoons oil over medium heat in dutch oven. Stir in ½ cup onions;

cook for 5 minutes until softened. Raise heat to high and stir in millet. Continue stirring and cook for about 5 minutes, until mixture darkens and smells nutty. Add 2 cups stock and bring to boil. Reduce heat to low; simmer covered for 20 minutes or until liquid is absorbed. Remove from heat. Cook remaining oil and onions in large saucepan over medium heat, stirring for 7 to 8 minutes until softened. Add squash, sweet potatoes, paprika, cumin, ginger, and cinnamon. Cook for 1 minute. Stir in remaining stock; cover and simmer for 12 to 15 minutes until vegetables are softened. Add cooked vegetable spice mixture to millet mixture in dutch oven. Add salt to taste. Either transfer dutch oven to oven or turn millet vegetable mixture into buttered 3-quart baking dish. Bake at 400 degrees for 20 minutes. Yield: 6 to 8 servings

Sweet and Sour Red Cabbage

4 tablespoons oil or butter
1 large sweet onion, finely chopped
2 large apples, peeled and chopped
1 (2½ to 3 pounds) red cabbage,
   shredded
1 bay leaf
⅓ cup honey

2 tablespoons lemon juice
½ teaspoon salt
½ teaspoon pepper
⅛ teaspoon ground cloves
3 cups water
½ cup cider vinegar

Heat oil in large skillet or dutch oven over medium heat. Add onion and apples and cook for 2 to 3 minutes, stirring constantly. Stir in cabbage, bay leaf, honey, lemon juice, salt, pepper, and cloves. Toss ingredients to thoroughly blend. Stir in water and vinegar. Cover; cook over low heat for about 1 to 1½ hours, until cabbage is tender. Stir occasionally. Yield: 6 servings

Notes

··

··

··

··

··

··

Fruit Salads

Apple Poinsettia Salads

1½ cups water
1 cup sugar
6 very thin lemon slices
¼ cup red cinnamon candies

6 medium apples, peeled and cored
8 circular pineapple slices
1 hard-cooked egg yolk

In saucepan, bring water, sugar, lemon, and cinnamon candies to a boil. Slice each apple into 8 lengthwise slices. Add slices to syrup. Simmer slowly until apples are tender but firm, about 10 minutes. Refrigerate slices in syrup until serving time. Drain slices from syrup just before serving. Place a pineapple slice on plate. Arrange 6 apple slices on top of pineapple to form poinsettia flower petals. Rub egg yolk through a sieve; sprinkle a bit in center of apple slices. Repeat until all salads are made. Yield: 8 servings

Orange Shell Salads

4 oranges
½ cup orange pulp
1½ cups fruit cocktail, drained
¼ cup blanched almonds, chopped
6 ounces cream cheese, softened
¼ cup mayonnaise

1 tablespoon vinegar
¼ teaspoon prepared yellow mustard
⅛ teaspoon salt
½ cup heavy whipping cream
2 tablespoons slivered almonds, toasted

Wash oranges; cut each in half. Scoop out pulp; discard pith and seeds; reserve shells. Dice pulp. In bowl, combine ½ cup pulp with fruit cocktail and almonds. In small bowl, mix cream cheese, mayonnaise, vinegar, mustard, and salt. Add to fruit mixture. With electric mixer, whip cream until stiff. Fold in fruit mixture. Divide salad evenly into the orange shells. At this point salads can be refrigerated and served the same day or frozen for 3 months till needed.

Two Sweet Potato Bakes

Orange Sweet Potato Bake

3 pounds sweet potatoes
Zest of 1 orange
2 large eggs, well beaten
½ cup brown sugar
½ cup molasses

⅓ cup orange juice
½ cup butter, softened
½ teaspoon ground nutmeg
½ teaspoon ground cloves
½ teaspoon ground allspice

Preheat oven to 325 degrees. Butter 2-quart baking dish; set aside. Wash, peel, and grate sweet potatoes. Combine sweet potatoes and orange zest in bowl; set aside. With electric mixer, beat eggs, brown sugar, and molasses together until smooth and creamy. Add sweet potato orange mixture. Stir in juice, butter, nutmeg, cloves, and allspice, mixing until thoroughly combined. Spoon sweet potato mixture into prepared baking dish. Bake for 50 to 60 minutes. This dish can be served hot or cold. Yield: 8 to 10 servings

Sweet Potato Apple Bake

1 pound sweet potatoes
1¼ pounds apples
6 tablespoons butter, cut up into small pieces

1 teaspoon salt
½ cup brown sugar
1 teaspoon ground nutmeg
1 tablespoon lemon juice

Preheat oven to 400 degrees. Butter a baking dish; set aside. Wash, peel, and thinly slice sweet potatoes. Peel, core, and thinly slice apples. Beginning and ending with layer of sweet potato slices, layer sweet potatoes, apples, a tiny piece of butter, salt, brown sugar, nutmeg, and lemon juice. Dot top with remaining butter. Bake for 40 to 50 minutes or until potato slices are tender. Yield: 6 servings

Roast Mixed Vegetables

3 pounds potatoes
4 rutabagas or turnips
6 parsnips
12 carrots
12 brussels sprouts
1 medium-size winter squash
  (hubbard, butternut, acorn)
6 sweet onions

6 to 8 cloves garlic
2 bay leaves
¼ cup beef drippings or olive oil
2 teaspoons dried thyme, rosemary, sage,
  or parsley
Kosher salt to taste
Freshly ground peppercorns to taste
1 head cauliflower florets

Preheat oven to 425 degrees. Spray shallow roasting pan with nonstick cooking spray; set aside. Wash, peel, and quarter potatoes and rutabagas. With tines of fork, lightly score all sides of potatoes and rutabagas. Wash, trim, and peel parsnips and carrots. Trim sprouts and cut them in half. Peel, seed, and cut winter squash into large cubes. Trim and peel onions and quarter them. Trim and peel garlic cloves and leave them whole. Place vegetables in roasting pan, mixing them well. Place bay leaves in with vegetables. In small bowl, stir together drippings or oil, the herb of your choice, salt, and pepper. Pour mixture over vegetables, stirring to cover pieces of vegetables. Cover and roast for 20 minutes. Uncover, add the cauliflower florets, and roast 20 to 30 minutes longer, stirring occasionally, until tender. Remove bay leaves and transfer vegetables to warm serving dish. Yield: 8 to 10 servings

Notes

Twice-Baked Rolls or Breads

Make and freeze these rolls or breads up to 3 months in advance. When needed, thaw and pop them in the oven for homemade goodness in short order.

1 package dry yeast
½ cup lukewarm water, heated to
 110 degrees
½ tablespoon sugar
2½ teaspoons salt

⅛ cup sugar
1 cup scalded milk
5 cups flour, approximate, divided
¼ cup butter or shortening, melted,
 cooled

Dissolve yeast in lukewarm water; add ½ tablespoon sugar. Combine salt and remaining sugar in bowl; add milk, stirring to dissolve. Cool to lukewarm; add yeast mixture. Mix in half the flour; add butter; beat until smooth. Add enough remaining flour to make soft dough. On lightly floured board, knead dough until smooth and satiny. Place dough in greased bowl; roll dough to grease all sides. Cover with damp towel. Let rise in warm place until doubled. Punch down. Knead again on floured board. Divide into 4 portions. Cover with damp towel for 20 minutes. Preheat oven to 275 degrees. Shape into 2 to 3 dozen rolls or 2 loaves.* Place rolls on baking sheets, loaves in well-greased 5x9-inch pans. Let rise in warm place until ¾ as high as regular rolls or bread. Bake rolls 40 minutes, bread 75 minutes. Let rolls and bread cool in pans 20 minutes before transferring to wire racks to cool completely. Wrap; freeze up to 3 months. Yield: 2 to 3 dozen rolls; 2 bread loaves

To serve, place rolls or loaves on ungreased baking sheet; thaw. Preheat oven to 450 degrees; bake 7 minutes.

*NOTE: To make cinnamon bread: Shape dough portions into 6x10-inch rectangles ½-inch thick. Brush with melted butter, sprinkle ½ cup sugar and 2 teaspoons cinnamon over dough. Roll up, flatten ends, turn under; pinch to seal. Place in pan. Continue as per recipe.

Confection Celebration: Desserts

One great part of holiday celebrations usually comes near the end of the party: dessert! And for many of us, the cookies, cakes, pies, and puddings of Christmas hold a special nostalgic place in our heart. One way to incorporate special desserts at your party is to ask each family group to bring a treat that they hold dear. Maybe it's a type of cookie that they have always decorated together as a family, or maybe it's a cake that they make every year to celebrate the birth of Jesus. Some families have traditions of baking inedible objects (like a toothpick) into a dessert, and the person who ends up with that object has to do the dishes (just nibble carefully)! These special desserts will be wonderful conversation starters for you and your guests.

Without the door let sorrow lie,
And if for cold it chance to die,
We'll bury it in Christmas pie,
And evermore be merry!

ENGLISH TRADITIONAL CAROL

Angel Food Squares

*This easy dessert is a big hit with kids of all ages. Some suggestions
have been given below for toppings, but your imagination is the limit.*

1 (14 ounce) can sweetened condensed milk
1 cup marshmallow crème
1 teaspoon vanilla, almond, orange, or peppermint extract
1 baked and cooled angel food cake, cut into 1-inch squares
8 (1 ounce) squares chocolate, dark, milk, or semisweet, melted, optional
Toppings: finely ground nuts, flaked or toasted coconut, jimmies or sprinkles,
   chopped candied fruit, finely shaved chocolate, sifted cocoa powder

To make frosting, whip together milk, marshmallow crème, and extract
   of your choice until texture is smooth and creamy. Dip cake squares into

frosting. With small spoon, drizzle some chocolate on squares, if desired. Decorate cake squares with toppings of your choice. Transfer cake squares to wire rack to set up. The cake squares can be made ahead and frozen. Just bring them to room temperature before serving. Yield: 5 to 6 dozen cake squares

Another way to serve these squares is to assemble all the ingredients separately on a small table. Include plenty of dipping forks, party picks, small spoons, and small plates beside unfrosted cake squares, frosting, melted chocolate, and toppings. Invite your guests to frost cake squares with frosting and their favorite toppings.

Notes

Ruth's Praline Wafer Dessert

45 vanilla wafer cookies
½ cup flaked coconut
⅓ cup finely chopped pecans
⅓ cup brown sugar, packed
3 tablespoons butter

1 (3.4 ounce) package instant vanilla
   pudding mix
1½ cups milk
1 cup heavy cream, whipped to stiff peaks

Arrange 21 whole cookies in bottom of 9-inch or 10-inch springform pan. Cut a straight edge on the rest of the cookies and arrange around the sides in the pan. Set aside.

Combine coconut, pecans, sugar, and butter in saucepan. Cook on low heat, stirring until butter is melted. Cook 5 minutes or until mixture browns slightly. Pour mixture onto greased baking sheet to cool. When cooled, break up into coarse crumbs. Set aside ½ cup praline crumbs. Sprinkle rest of praline crumbs over cookies in base of springform pan.

Prepare pudding with milk as directed on package. Fold in whipping cream. Spoon this mixture into pan, spreading gently to edges of cookies. Sprinkle reserved praline crumbs on top of dessert. They can be sprinkled evenly over top or in a pattern or design. Chill overnight or at least 4 hours before serving.

Notes

Cream Cheese Shells

½ cup butter, softened   1 cup flour
3 ounces cream cheese, softened

Lightly grease cups of two mini-muffin pans; set aside. In bowl, beat butter and cream cheese until thoroughly blended; beat in flour. Drop dough by tablespoonfuls into prepared muffin cups. Press dough onto bottom and sides of each cup. Repeat this process until all cups are filled. Bake at 325 degrees for 20 to 25 minutes or until lightly golden brown. Cool for 5 minutes before removing to wire rack to cool. Yield: 24 shells

Notes

....

....

....

....

....

....

....

Susannah's Holiday Nut Roll

The dough and filling may be used to make one large nut roll, or divided in half to form two smaller ones. The baking time is the same for both.

1 cake fresh yeast or 1 package dry yeast
1 cup lukewarm milk, heated to
   110 degrees, divided
¼ cup sugar, divided

1½ teaspoons salt
2 large eggs, beaten
3½ cups flour, sifted, divided
⅓ cup butter, melted

FILLING:
6 egg whites, well beaten
1 cup finely ground walnuts
1 cup sugar

Dissolve yeast in ¼ cup lukewarm milk, adding 1 teaspoon sugar; let stand

and rise for at least 5 minutes. Combine softened yeast with remaining milk and sugar, salt, and eggs. Blend well. Add half of flour and beat until smooth. Add remaining flour and mix to a soft dough. Knead and beat air into dough until bubbles are formed. Cover; let rise until doubled in bulk. Roll into rectangle on floured board to ½-inch thickness. FILLING: Spread egg whites over dough. Cover evenly with nuts and sugar. Starting at one short end of dough, roll like a jelly roll. Place roll or rolls on greased baking sheet. Let rise until doubled in bulk. Bake at 375 degrees for about 35 minutes or until golden brown.

Notes

....

....

Chocolate Chestnut Roll

½ cup flour
¼ cup unsweetened cocoa powder
1 teaspoon baking powder
4 large eggs, separated
¾ cup sugar
1 teaspoon pure vanilla extract
2 tablespoons water
Powdered sugar, for dusting

1 (15.5 ounce) can chestnut puree
¼ cup heavy cream
¼ cup powdered sugar
1 tablespoon pure vanilla extract
1 cup heavy cream
2 tablespoons unsweetened cocoa powder
1 tablespoon powdered sugar

Grease 15½x10½x1-inch jelly roll pan; line with parchment paper and grease paper. Sift together flour, cocoa, and baking powder; set aside. Beat yolks in large bowl until fluffy; gradually add sugar; beat until very thick. Stir in vanilla and water. Fold in flour mixture; set aside. Beat egg whites until stiff glossy peaks form. Gently fold into batter. The whites should be thoroughly dispersed throughout batter. Spread into prepared pan. Bake at 375 degrees for 12 minutes or until center springs back when lightly touched. Dust with powdered sugar; cover with tea towel and turn cake over. Remove pan and parchment paper. Using a sharp serrated knife, trim ¼ inch from each side of cake. Starting at one short end of cake, tightly roll up cake and towel; place it seam edge down on wire rack to cool. While cake is cooling, make chestnut filling and cocoa frosting.

Beat chestnut puree until smooth and spreadable; set aside. Beat ¼ cup heavy cream, ¼ cup powdered sugar, and vanilla until stiff. Fold in chestnut puree; set aside.

To make frosting, beat 1 cup heavy cream, cocoa powder, and powdered sugar until stiff. When cake is cool, unroll; spread chestnut filling over cake. Roll cake, without the towel; frost. Refrigerate. Yield: 10 to 12 servings

Pumpkin Praline Layer Cake

2 cups flour
2 teaspoons baking powder
1 teaspoon baking soda
2 teaspoons pumpkin pie spice
1 teaspoon salt
4 large eggs
1⅓ cups sugar
1 cup vegetable oil
1 (15 ounce) can pumpkin puree
  or homemade equivalent

¼ teaspoon pure vanilla extract
¾ cup brown sugar, packed
⅓ cup unsalted butter
3 tablespoons heavy whipping cream
¾ cup chopped pecans
1¾ cups heavy whipping cream
¼ cup powdered sugar
¼ teaspoon pure vanilla extract

Lightly grease two 9x1½-inch round cake pans; set aside. Preheat oven to 350 degrees. Sift together flour, baking powder, baking soda, pumpkin pie spice, and salt; set aside. Beat eggs, sugar, and oil at medium speed with electric mixer. Add pumpkin and vanilla, beating until well blended. Gradually combine dry ingredients into pumpkin mixture, beating until smooth. Divide batter evenly between the two prepared cake pans. Bake for 30 to 35 minutes or until pick inserted in center comes out clean. Transfer pans to wire racks and cool for 5 minutes. Remove cakes from pans and return to wire racks to cool completely. While cakes are cooling, cook brown sugar, butter, and 3 tablespoons heavy cream in saucepan over low heat, stirring until sugar is dissolved. Remove from heat and stir in chopped pecans. Spoon half of praline mixture on top of one cake layer; place the second layer on top of the first and spoon remaining praline on it. Make frosting by beating 1¾ cups heavy whipping cream with electric mixer until soft peaks form. Add sugar and vanilla, beating until blended. Spread frosting over top and sides of cake. Keep refrigerated.

Pistachio Cake

3 cups flour
2 cups sugar
½ cup nonfat dry milk powder
1 tablespoon baking powder
½ teaspoon salt
2 (1.5 ounce) boxes instant pistachio
  pudding mix, divided
3 large eggs
1 teaspoon pure vanilla extract

1 cup vegetable oil
1 cup ginger ale
½ cup chopped nuts (pistachios, pecans,
  walnuts, hazelnuts)
1 cup heavy whipping cream
1 cup milk
¼ cup chopped nuts (pistachios, pecans,
  walnuts, hazelnuts), for topping

Lightly grease and flour angel food or tube cake pan; set aside. Preheat oven to
350 degrees. In large mixing bowl, sift together flour, sugar, nonfat milk
powder, baking powder, and salt. With electric mixer, blend in 1 box of

pudding mix, eggs, vanilla, oil, and ginger ale. Beat for 2 minutes on medium speed. Stir in ½ cup chopped nuts. Pour batter into prepared cake pan. Bake for 50 to 60 minutes or until pick inserted in center of cake comes out clean. Transfer cake pan to wire rack to cool for at least 25 minutes. Remove cake from pan and return to wire rack to cool completely.

When completely cooled, split cake in half or thirds horizontally to make layers; set aside. Make frosting by whisking heavy whipping cream, milk, and remaining box of pudding mix until stiff peaks form. Spread frosting between layers and over top and sides of cake. Sprinkle remaining chopped nuts over top of cake. Keep refrigerated.

ELEGANT FRESH FRUIT DESSERTS

Pears with Chocolate Sauce

2 cups water
1 cup sugar
1 cinnamon stick
1 tablespoon lemon zest
Juice of half a lemon

6 ripe pears
6 (1 ounce) squares semisweet chocolate
2 tablespoons unsalted butter
1 cup heavy whipping cream
1 teaspoon pure vanilla extract

In saucepan combine sugar, water, cinnamon stick, lemon zest, and juice over medium heat. Bring to a boil. Reduce heat and simmer for 5 minutes. As each pear is peeled, lower it into gently simmering syrup. Poach pears for 20 minutes. Remove pears from heat and let cool while making chocolate sauce.

Coarsely chop chocolate squares. Place chocolate, butter, and heavy cream in small saucepan. Stirring constantly, heat over low heat until chocolate has completely melted. Remove from heat and stir in vanilla. Place each pear on individual dessert plate. Spoon chocolate sauce over and around pears. Yield: 6 servings

Figs with Orange Syrup

1 orange
½ cup sugar
¼ cup water

1 tablespoon orange extract or flavoring
1 tablespoon almond extract or flavoring
16 fresh figs

With sharp knife, remove a thin strip of rind from orange, removing all white pith. Juice orange. Place strip of rind and juice in saucepan. Stir in sugar and water. Bring to a boil; reduce heat and cook until syrup is thick and bubbly. Cool slightly. Remove orange rind and stir in orange and almond extracts. Cut figs in half; place 4 fig halves into each individual dessert dish. Spoon syrup over figs. Cover and refrigerate until serving. Yield: 8 servings

Kellie's Spicy Pumpkin Cheesecake

No one will ever know this delicious treat is dairy-free.
It receives rave reviews whenever it is served.

1½ cups graham cracker crumbs
4 tablespoons pure maple syrup
½ tablespoon oil
1 (12 ounce) package firm tofu, pureed
1 (8 ounce) package soy cream-style
  cheese, softened and pureed
1 cup plain pumpkin puree
1 cup unrefined cane sugar

3 tablespoons flour
1½ teaspoons ground cinnamon
½ teaspoon ground ginger
½ teaspoon ground nutmeg
½ teaspoon ground allspice
2 tablespoons molasses
⅛ teaspoon salt
¼ teaspoon baking soda

Preheat oven to 350 degrees. Spray 9-inch or 10-inch springform pan with nonstick cooking spray. In small bowl, combine graham cracker crumbs, maple syrup, and oil. Press crumb mixture into bottom of prepared pan. With food processor, puree tofu, cream-style cheese, and pumpkin puree until mixture is very smooth. Transfer pureed mixture to large bowl if food processor bowl is not large enough to hold all ingredients. Alternately beat tofu, cream-style cheese, and pumpkin puree with electric mixer until texture is very smooth. Add remaining ingredients in order listed, blending well to make sure all are incorporated. Pour pumpkin mixture into pan, spreading top evenly. Bake for 50 minutes. Cool for 30 minutes. Refrigerate for 5 to 6 hours or overnight before serving.

Lemon Tart

2 small lemons
1 (8 inch) tart shell, unbaked
1 tablespoon flour
⅓ cup ground almonds
4 tablespoons butter

4 tablespoons sugar
Zest of 1 lemon
1 large egg
⅛ teaspoon pure vanilla extract
1 cup sugar

Wash lemons thoroughly. Cut into slices ⅛-inch thick. Carefully remove seeds. Place slices in a bowl; cover with boiling water. Soak slices for 8 hours; drain. Place slices in saucepan; add just enough cold water to cover. Heat until boiling rapidly; reduce heat; put a lid on saucepan. Simmer 30 minutes or until rinds are soft and flesh almost disintegrated. Remove from heat; set aside to let slices cool in liquid. Prick bottom of tart shell lightly with fork. Line shell with foil and pie weights; bake at 375 degrees for 5 minutes. Remove foil and pie weights; set aside. In bowl, mix together flour and almonds; set aside. Cream butter and 4 tablespoons sugar until soft and light. Blend in lemon zest. Gradually stir in egg and combined flour and almonds, stirring to thoroughly blend. Spread this mixture over bottom of tart shell. Bake at 375 degrees 25 to 30 minutes or until tart has risen, is golden and firm to the touch. Transfer to wire rack to cool completely. Reserving 1 cup liquid, drain lemon slices. In saucepan, combine 1 cup reserved liquid, vanilla, and 1 cup sugar over low heat until sugar has dissolved. Add lemon slices; simmer gently 5 minutes. Remove slices and place in tart shell in circular pattern. Continue boiling until syrup reaches 220 degrees. Remove syrup from heat; when syrup stops bubbling, spoon over lemon slices. Refrigerate until cold before serving. Yield: 8 servings

Pie in a Pumpkin

1 (5 to 7 pound) whole pie pumpkin*
6 large eggs
2 cups heavy whipping cream
½ cup brown sugar, packed
1 tablespoon maple syrup, molasses,
  or honey

½ teaspoon freshly grated nutmeg
1 teaspoon ground cinnamon
¼ teaspoon ground ginger
¼ teaspoon pure vanilla extract
2 tablespoons unsalted butter,
  cut into small pieces

Wash pumpkin. Cut off top and set aside. Remove seeds and strings from center of pumpkin. Place pumpkin in lightly buttered large shallow baking dish. Preheat oven to 350 degrees. With electric mixer, beat eggs, heavy cream, sugar, syrup, nutmeg, cinnamon, ginger, and vanilla. Fill pumpkin with custard. Dot top of custard with butter. Place top on pumpkin. Bake pumpkin for 1 to 2 hours or until custard is set. Remove pumpkin from oven. To serve pie in a pumpkin, scoop up some of cooked pumpkin with custard for each serving. Yield: 8 servings

NOTE: Make individual pies by using 8 small pie pumpkins or sweet dumpling squash instead of the larger pumpkin. Prepare recipe as above; dividing the custard evenly. Bake pumpkins at 350 degrees for 45 to 60 minutes or until custard is set.

Notes

Pecan Cake Rolls

1½ tablespoons unsalted butter, melted
6 large eggs, separated
½ cup sugar
Pinch of salt
1 cup finely ground pecans

1 cup heavy cream
2 tablespoons sugar
½ teaspoon pure vanilla extract
½ cup finely ground pecans

Preheat oven to 400 degrees. Brush melted butter over bottom of 15½x10½x1-inch jelly roll pan; line bottom with parchment or waxed paper and grease paper. Do not grease sides of pan. Set aside. Beat egg yolks, ½ cup sugar, and pinch of salt in large bowl until light and a lemony color. Fold in 1 cup pecans; set aside. Beat egg whites until stiff peaks form. Gently but quickly fold whites into egg and sugar mixture. The whites should be thoroughly dispersed throughout batter. Spread batter evenly into prepared pan. Bake for 15 to 18 minutes or until center springs back when lightly touched. Turn baked cake over onto sheet of parchment or waxed paper. Immediately remove pan and paper adhering to cake. Allow cake to cool. With electric mixer, beat heavy cream until stiff. Add 2 tablespoons sugar and vanilla. Fold in remaining ground pecans. Spread sweetened whipped cream over cake evenly. Starting at one short end of cake, tightly roll up cake. Place it seam edge down. Refrigerate. Slice into 1-inch-thick slices before serving. Yield: 8 to 10 servings

Notes

Dad's Favorite Coconut Cream Pie

¾ cup sugar
7 tablespoons flour
¼ teaspoon salt
2 large eggs
3 cups milk, scalded, divided*
1 teaspoon pure vanilla extract
¾ to 1 cup coconut, shredded or flaked

1 9-inch pie crust (baked and cooled
   pastry or graham cracker)
2 large egg whites for meringue
2 to 4 tablespoons sugar for meringue
Sweetened whipped cream, optional
Toasted coconut, shredded or flaked,
   optional

In large saucepan, whisk together sugar, flour, salt, and eggs. Add 1 or 2 tablespoons of scalded milk to egg mixture, whisking constantly. Gradually add remaining scalded milk while still whisking. Heat mixture on low heat, stirring constantly until it begins to boil. Reduce heat to low and simmer.

While stirring, cook for 2 to 3 minutes. Remove saucepan from heat. Stir in vanilla. Allow mixture to cool to room temperature. Fold in coconut. Pour filling into prepared pie shell. Here are 2 toppings for this pie.

Method 1: Meringue: With electric mixer, beat egg whites and 4 tablespoons sugar together until stiff peaks form. Spoon meringue over pie, making sure meringue covers contents of pie and touches pie shell all around to prevent meringue from shrinking. Use back of a spoon or a spatula to make decorative peaks in meringue. Preheat oven to 350 degrees; bake 15 to 20 minutes.

Method 2: Whipped cream and coconut: Spoon, or using a pastry bag, pipe sweetened whipped cream over top of pie; sprinkle toasted coconut over surface. Refrigerate until serving.

NOTE: Use milk, cream, evaporated milk, unsweetened coconut milk, or a combination of milks.

Chocolate Crème Brûlée

This rich dessert can be made up to 2 days in advance.

3 cups heavy whipping cream
8 (1 ounce) squares semisweet chocolate,
    chopped
1 teaspoon pure vanilla extract
⅛ teaspoon ground cinnamon
8 large egg yolks

½ cup sugar
¼ cup brown sugar, packed
Fresh fruit, optional for topping
Sweetened whipped cream, optional for
    topping

Preheat oven to 325 degrees. Spray 8 ramekins with nonstick cooking spray; set aside. In saucepan over low heat, whisk together heavy cream, chopped chocolate, vanilla, and cinnamon. Cook until smooth. Remove from heat; set aside. In mixing bowl, whisk egg yolks and sugar until smooth. Add 1 or 2 tablespoons of chocolate mixture to egg yolks, whisking constantly. Gradually add remaining chocolate mixture while still whisking. Cool mixture slightly. Divide mixture evenly into prepared ramekins. Place ramekins in a baking dish with deep sides. Place baking dish on center oven rack. Pour hot water into baking dish; be careful not to get water in ramekins. The hot water should come halfway up sides of ramekins. Bake custard for 50 minutes or until firm in the center. Remove from oven and remove ramekins from baking dish. Transfer ramekins to wire racks to cool completely. Refrigerate until well chilled. About 1 hour before serving, heat broiler. Sprinkle brown sugar on top of each ramekin. Place ramekins under broiler to caramelize sugar. Transfer ramekins to wire racks to cool. Refrigerate until serving. If desired, just before serving, top each brûlée with fresh fruit and/or sweetened whipped cream. Yield: 8 servings

Pineapple Cake

9 large eggs
1½ cups sugar
1 teaspoon lemon extract

1 cup flour
4 tablespoons cornstarch
3 tablespoons butter, melted

FROSTING:
1 cup sugar
½ cup water
3 large egg yolks
1 cup butter, softened

3 tablespoons pineapple juice
¾ cup finely chopped fresh pineapple
6 slices fresh pineapple, peeled, cored,
   quartered

Preheat oven to 350 degrees. Lightly grease two 9-inch round cake pans; dust
with flour; set aside. Combine eggs and sugar in large bowl held over a pan
of hot water; do not heat. Whisk until sugar dissolves. Beat in extract; discard

pan of hot water. With electric mixer, beat mixture on high speed until cool, pale colored, and volume has tripled. Sift together flour and cornstarch. Add one-third of dry ingredients at a time, folding each addition into batter. Fold in melted butter. Divide batter evenly into prepared pans. Bake 20 minutes or until cake tester in center comes out clean. Transfer pans to wire racks to cool 10 minutes; remove cakes from pans; place cakes on wire racks to cool completely. FROSTING: Combine sugar and water in saucepan, bringing mixture to a boil over medium heat. Cook until candy thermometer registers 240 degrees. Place egg yolks in bowl; beat with electric mixer until thick and pale colored. Still beating yolks, add hot syrup; continue beating until mixture is cool, pale, and thick. In another bowl, beat softened butter until creamy. Gradually beat butter into egg yolk mixture. Stir in pineapple juice. Mix 1 cup frosting with chopped pineapple; spread over top of one cake layer. Position second layer on top; refrigerate 15 minutes. When filling has set, frost entire cake. Refrigerate 15 minutes. Before serving, decorate with pineapple slices.

Creative Christmas: Favors, Decorating Ideas, Party Games

Christmas is a time for merriment and cheer, but that doesn't mean that you have to celebrate the same way year after year! Here are some creative and fun ideas to incorporate into your next get-together. Remember that these are just starting points. Feel free to take these ideas and make them your own!

At Christmas, play and make good cheer,
For Christmas comes but once a year.

THOMAS TUSSER, 16TH CENTURY

Notes

....

....

....

....

....

....

....

SIMPLE DECORATING

Crystal and Ornaments

ITEMS NEEDED:
Crystal bowl
Round red ornaments

Fill a crystal bowl with bright red round ornaments. This makes a stunning centerpiece or accent for any room. Experiment with clear vases and other ornaments, too!

Candy Canes

Candy canes are always a wonderful and versatile decoration at Christmas. Tie with bows and use as place settings. Hang them on your tree. Place in a vase or large bowl. Attach them to gifts.

Consider printing out a scripture verse such as one of the following and attaching to the candy with ribbon:

Now all this was done, that it might be fulfilled which was spoken of the Lord by the prophet, saying, Behold, a virgin shall be with child, and shall bring forth a son, and they shall call his name Emmanuel, which being interpreted is, God with us.
MATTHEW 1:22–23

Live Rosemary Centerpiece

*Here's a festive decorating idea that will incorporate a "Christmas tree"
into the dining area—an area of the house that isn't usually
large enough to accommodate a full-size tree.*

Purchase a miniature rosemary plant that has been shaped like a Christmas
tree. Set this in the middle of your table and decorate. Use silver or gold
ornaments for a more elegant look or have your children make their own
ornaments for a fun Christmas project.

Real rosemary plants need six to eight hours of sunlight and need to be
kept warm. They are fairly easy to care for. Make sure your dining room table
gets plenty of light if that is where you'll be keeping your rosemary "tree."

Water well when the soil dries, but allow to dry in between watering.

Uses for rosemary (after the holiday season):

Cooking	Floral arrangements
Baking	Potpourri
Insect repellent	Medicinal tea
Wreaths	

*And she brought forth her firstborn son, and wrapped
him in swaddling clothes, and laid him in a manger.*
LUKE 2:7

*When they were come into the house, they saw the young child
with Mary his mother, and fell down, and worshipped him.*
MATTHEW 2:11

A "Scrambled" Dinner Party

Invite about eight friends over for a casual dinner. Assign each couple one side dish recipe you plan to serve (enough for each guest to have a small serving). That's all they need to know. The host provides an entrée and dessert, but your guests won't have any idea what you're serving or what anyone else is bringing.

The night of the party, there are no place settings; the only items for each guest are a menu and a pen. Create the menus by folding paper in half like a greeting card. When opened, the left side of the menu will be a list of every item on the menu (including eating utensils, each individual dish, and beverage), but each will be cleverly disguised under a new name. Mashed potatoes become "Clouds over Bethlehem," and a butter knife is "Herod's

Scepter." If your main dish is beef, you might call it "Cattle Are Lowing," a napkin is "Swaddling Clothes," and so on—pull out all your creative genius for this! The right side of the menu contains blank lines under the headings of COURSE I, COURSE II, COURSE III, one line for each item that will be served from the left side of the menu. Have guests fill out all three courses at once, then write their names at the top and turn them in to servers.

You will need help in the kitchen for this event, so ask a few of the members of the church youth group to come help out for this fun evening. They will be filling orders, serving, and clearing after each course. (Forget the good china and use fun holiday paper products and plastic utensils for quick cleanup.)

The fun really starts when Course I appears: Someone gets a vegetable, dessert, and meat but didn't order a fork, so she only has a toothpick to eat it with! Someone else has unwittingly ordered a napkin, a glass of water, and all his silverware for Course I and has to eat his next two courses with his fingers!

When the meal is over, invite guests to finish off any of the food, drink, and dessert left in the kitchen, this time filling their own plates.

Cookie Recipe Favors

Here's a simple party favor that is sure to bring a smile to your guests' faces. Everyone loves the fun and festive shapes of cutout cookies!

ITEMS NEEDED:
3x5-inch index cards
Colorful ink pens
Cookie cutters

Hole punch
Ribbon

Write out your favorite Christmas cutout cookie recipe with colored pens. Or if you are having a large number of guests, print out recipes from your computer and attach to recipe cards with glue or clear tape. Punch a hole in each recipe card and attach a cookie cutter with a colorful ribbon to give to each guest as a party favor. For an added personal touch, visit a kitchen store and pick out unique cookie-cutter shapes for each guest, based on his or her interests. For example, give a dog lover a dog bone–shaped cutter. For a musical person, give a music note–shaped cutter.

Then be ye glad, good people,
This night of all the year,
And light ye up your candles:
His star is drawing near.

TRADITIONAL CAROL

Name That Tune

ITEMS NEEDED:
Christmas music
CD or cassette player
Notepad

Pencil
Scorekeeper

....

Select ten popular Christmas songs and play just a small portion of the song or edit snippets of the songs in various places. The first person to call out the right answer gets a point. Whoever gets the most songs right wins. Play just for fun or for a prize.

Select a mix of traditional Christmas carols and popular Christmas songs ranging from easy to difficult. Here are some ideas to keep everyone guessing:

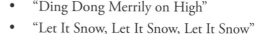

- "Ding Dong Merrily on High"
- "Let It Snow, Let It Snow, Let It Snow"
- "The Twelve Days of Christmas"
- "Angels We Have Heard on High"
- "Joy to the World"
- "Sleigh Ride"
- "I'll Be Home for Christmas"
- "Winter Wonderland"
- "The Little Drummer Boy"

Pass the Stocking

ITEMS NEEDED:
1 large Christmas stocking
5 to 10 small household items (measuring
    cup, thread bobbin, roll of tape, coaster,
    etc.)

Paper for each guest
Pen/pencil for each guest
Timer

Fill a stocking with household items. Pass the stocking around and allow each guest to feel it for thirty seconds without looking inside. Have guests write down as many items as they can guess. Whoever guesses the most correct answers wins a prize.

Did You Know?

There seems to be no official documentation or date of when the Christmas stocking tradition started, but more of a legend that has been passed down from generation to generation. The legend differs in various countries, but the basis is that the daughters of a poor family left their stockings out to dry over the fireplace. Saint Nicholas heard of their suffering and decided to help them. When the family woke the next morning, the stockings were full of gold and gifts. Christmas stockings became a more widespread tradition in 1822 when a poet named Clement Clark Moore wrote "A Visit from St. Nicholas" including the now well-known words: "The stockings were hung by the chimney with care."

Christmas House-Making Contest

ITEMS NEEDED:

Graham crackers
Colored icing
Toothpicks
Licorice
Small candies

Sprinkles, etc.
Utensils
Paper
Pens/pencils

Have each guest create a Christmas house. Number each house and have each guest vote on the winner. If there are many entries, you could have categories such as tallest, most creative, most whimsical, most icing used, etc.

Did You Know?

Gingerbread houses became popular after the fairy tale "Hansel and Gretel" was written. The largest gingerbread house was built in 2006 inside the Mall of America. The house was 67 feet tall, took over 1,700 hours to build, and used nearly 5,000 pounds of icing and over 14,000 pounds of gingerbread!

Notes

DECORATING 101

Pinecones and Berries

Pinecones and berries on a platter or bowl make a beautiful and inexpensive decoration. Find pinecones outdoors and use cranberries or purchase artificial berries at a hobby store.

KID TIP: Allow kids to hunt for pinecones outside or at a local park. After you have picked out the nice ones to use indoors as decorations, allow children to decorate the remaining pinecones for the birds. Add peanut butter and sprinkle with birdseed and berries. Tie with red and green ribbon and attach to the trees and bushes outside.

Bead Garlands

Garlands aren't just for Christmas trees. Think outside the tree! Arrange red and silver bead garlands in bowls and vases and allow them to cascade over the edges. Sitting the bowls on top of mirrors adds extra sparkle. Garlands look great on tables, mantels, countertops, staircases, etc.

KID TIP: Kids can make their own garlands out of red and green paper. Cut strips of construction paper and attach with a glue stick. Make a special "countdown to Christmas" garland while you're at it. Start with one link on December 1st and add a new paper link every day until Christmas. Write a special prayer or scripture on each link before you glue it together.

Hide the Ornament

ITEMS NEEDED:
1 unique ornament

Several cultures have the tradition of hiding an ornament (like a pickle), on the Christmas tree, and the first person to find it receives a special present. For your party, consider hiding a unique (or silly) ornament somewhere in your house that guests will have access to. As people arrive, explain the game to them and describe the ornament that they will be looking for. As the evening progresses, if no one finds the ornament, you can start dropping subtle hints about where it might be. When someone finds the ornament, they should be declared the winner and given a prize. If the ornament itself is especially strange (and doesn't hold sentimental value to you or your family), you may consider giving the ornament to the winner, as it would make for a fun memory on their Christmas tree for years to come.

Did You Know?

The pickle ornament is a very old German Christmas tradition. The parents hung the pickle last after all the other ornaments were in place and would give an extra present to the most observant child who found the pickle first. Why a pickle? Nobody knows exactly, but a dark green vegetable hidden deep inside a dark green tree makes for a challenging game!

Blueberry Muffin Mix Favor

Jar mixes are a fun, useful, and delicious favor to send home with your guests. These muffins make a great breakfast.

1¾ cups flour
½ cup sugar

2 teaspoons baking powder
1 teaspoon dried, grated lemon peel

In medium bowl, combine all ingredients. Spoon muffin mix into 1-pint glass jar. Attach a recipe card with the following instructions (see next page).

Blueberry Muffin Mix

1 egg, slightly beaten
¾ cup milk

¼ cup vegetable oil
¾ cup fresh or frozen blueberries

Preheat oven to 400 degrees. Line muffin tin with paper baking cups. In large bowl, empty Blueberry Muffin Mix. Add egg, milk, and oil, stirring with a spoon until combined. Fold in blueberries. Pour batter into baking cups until two-thirds full. Bake for 20 minutes or until lightly golden. Remove muffins from tin to wire rack to cool slightly. Serve warm.

Triple Chocolate Chunk Cookie Mix

Send your guests home with the yumminess they just experienced at your party!
Everyone loves cookies, and chocolate makes everything better.

½ cup sugar
¾ cup packed brown sugar
1¾ cups all-purpose flour
1 teaspoon baking soda
½ teaspoon salt

⅓ cup unsweetened cocoa powder
4 ounces white chocolate chunks
½ cup milk chocolate chips
⅓ cup semisweet chocolate chips

In a 1-quart glass jar, layer ingredients in order given, combining flour, baking soda, and salt. Attach a recipe card with the following instructions (see next page).

Triple Chocolate Chunk Cookie Mix

1 cup butter, softened
1 teaspoon vanilla

2 eggs

Preheat oven to 325 degrees. Carefully remove semisweet chocolate chips, milk chocolate chips, and white chocolate chunks from Triple Chocolate Chunk Cookie Mix; set aside. In mixing bowl, beat butter, vanilla, and eggs until creamy. In large bowl, empty remaining contents of cookie mix, stirring to combine; add to creamed mixture until well blended. Stir in chocolate chips and white chocolate chunks. Drop by rounded tablespoonfuls onto ungreased cookie sheet. Bake 11 to 13 minutes or until cookies are set and appear dry. Cool 1 minute on cookie sheet before removing to wire rack.

Don't Say "Christmas"!

ITEMS NEEDED:
Safety pins
Christmas sequins, buttons,
  or small decorations

Craft glue

Decorate safety pins with small Christmas decorations or sequins. Give each guest a safety pin upon arrival. Explain the rules to each guest as they arrive. If anyone says the word *Christmas*, they have to give up their pin to the person who caught them. The guest with the most pins at the end of the party wins!

This game will be especially difficult with church friends, because Christians generally go out of their way to say "Merry Christmas" instead of

"Happy Holidays" this time of year. Remind yourself and others to spread joy and hope this Christmas to everyone they encounter, and try not to get caught up in the politics of Christmas. Wish others a hearty Merry Christmas, but do so out of love—not to force your own agenda.

Notes

Hot Potato Presents

ITEMS NEEDED:
1 prize
Lots of wrapping paper
Tape

Christmas music
CD player

Wrap one special prize with layers and layers of wrapping paper. Make it more difficult by using some packing or masking tape. Have guests sit in a circle and pass the gift around. As soon as the music stops, the person with the gift gets to unwrap as much as possible until the music starts again. Play until there is no more wrapping paper and the last person gets the prize.

Don't forget to honor the One whose birth and life we remember at

Christmas. Consider reading a devotion and scripture sometime during your party, or share the story of the magi and the first Christmas presents:

They departed; and lo, the star, which they saw in the east, went before them, till it came and stood over where the young child was. When they saw the star, they rejoiced with exceeding great joy. And when they were come into the house, they saw the young child with Mary his mother, and fell down, and worshipped him: and when they had opened their treasures, they presented unto him gifts; gold, and frankincense and myrrh.

MATTHEW 2:9–11